but, like others who have used mercenaries to extend their power, he found himself the puppet of those he paid. Ambrosius (Emrys) as a young man had warned Vortigern (Gwrtheyrn) that the Saxons would overrun the British lands and now he saw his fears confirmed. By 475 the Saxons occupied Sussex, Middlesex and Essex in the east and had advanced up the Thames from London into Berkshire, Oxfordshire and the Cotswolds, where the line was held by Ambrosius and his allies for a period of twenty years. The end of this phase of resistance was marked by the appearance of a great comet in 497, always a sign of impending catastrophe, as the priest Merlin confirmed when he declared that the great star signalled the death of Ambrosius.

It was at this point that a man called Arthur emerged as the new Pendragon, heir to Ambrosius and Uthyr Pendragon. It was this Arthur who was to defend the lands of the west for a further 30 years until his final defeat in 537. This was the Arthur with a court, Camelot, at Caerleon; with his 'knights', the surviving cavalry of the Romano-British nobility; with his broad-bladed battle sword Caledfwlch, known in legend as Excalibur; with his bards, his druids, his magicians; this was the 'Arthwyr of Briton' who stopped the Saxon advance at the Welsh borders to preserve a homeland for the Cymry, the British confederate tribes, which has survived in the legend and language of Wales to this day.

Left, is Llyn Barfog, the 'bearded lake', where Carn March Arthur (the stone of Arthur's stallion) bears the print of his horse's hoof with, above, the view from the lake to the Dovey estuary, home of the great bard Taliesin.

Who Was Merlin?

'THE BOY IS MYRDDIN AND THE MAN IS A KING CALLED GWRTHEYRN WHOM THE SAXONS CALL VORTIGERN.'

'I can see things others cannot. Beneath the mountains of Dinas Emrys I have seen two dragons, one red, one white ... The white dragon represents the Saxons and the red dragon represents the Britons. The white dragon is the stronger of the two but the red dragon will have his day ... There shall be a King after you who will drive out the Saxons and bring a time of peace and his name will be Arthur.'

A priest or druid called Myrddin often appears in early Arthurian stories. In Latin translations of these stories his name is Merlinus. Like the name Arthur, the name Merlin becomes a title attached to the greatest wizard or shaman of each generation, so that Merlin appears and reappears in different guises as he is literally reincarnated. Thus the young Ambrosius, Emrys Wledig, who warned Vortigern of the dangers in bringing Saxon mercenaries into the land, may be that same Myrddin Emrys who saw the white and red dragons fighting in Gwrtheyrn's Dinas Emrys and foretold the coming of Arthur.

The role of Merlin as a soothsayer and magician in this history is a reminder that myth and magic underpinned politics and war in the Dark Ages. That the legends of King Arthur are interwoven with myth and magic makes them more rather than less likely to be true. These were historical events related by Christian bards who still employed the language and imagery of pagan rituals and beliefs.

Dinas Emrys as it is today; the small hill seen across Llyn Dinas, near Beddgelert.

The Campaigns of King Arthur

'GIANTS AREN'T REAL ARE THEY? I THOUGHT ARTHUR WAS REAL.'
'Real enough to have stories told about him, and what better way of saying that Arthur had a large number of enemies than to give him one enemy who was very large. A giant. You see, stories don't have to be true, to be true, if you understand me.'

Arthur's battles were first recorded by a Welsh cleric Nennius in the *History of the Britons* which appeared around 830. Six battles were fought in the East Midlands against Anglo-Saxon raiders landing on the coast between the Humber and the Wash. The seventh and eighth battles seem to have been fought against the Picts crossing Hadrian's Wall in the borders of Scotland, suggesting that Arthur's alliance of Romano-British kings faced threats on several fronts. The remaining battles have all been located at the frontiers of Wales around the years 515 to 518: at Caerleon itself,

Aran Fawddwy and Benllyn from Bwlch-y-Groes. It is on this field that local legend says Arthur fought his great battle with Rhitta. The pass between Dinas Mawddwy and Bala might well have been the frontier of Rhitta's northern kingdom. Rhitta was said to be buried on Aran Benllyn, the mountain on the skyline, and this area is still known as Rhiw Barfau, the bearded hill.

'TELL ME YOUR STORY BRAN THE BLESSED'

'A long time ago, when I was King of the Island of the Mighty, my sister Branwen married an Irish King, Matholwch. He imprisoned her and treated her like a slave, and she sent for my help. I took a great army across the Irish sea. So large was I in life I simply waded across. There was a terrible battle which laid waste to both Kingdoms and I was struck by a poisoned spear.'

where the Silurian Arthur was said to have established his headquarters; on the banks of the Severn; and finally the battle of Badon near Bath, after which the Saxon advance was halted and there was a time of peace.

Accounts of these battles were preserved in oral history, in the stories and songs of the bards, and only later in written form. It is not surprising, then, that these stories and songs were embroidered into legend, and that the names of Arthur's enemies and the sites of his battles merged with local folklore. Among these legends in the Welsh tradition are tales of the battle with a rival warlord, the 'giant' Rhitta Fawr, and Arthur's rejection of the authority and laws of an earlier British king, Bendigeidfran, Bran the Blessed.

'ONCE THERE WAS A GIANT CALLED RHITTA ...'

'Now this Rhitta was King of North Wales, and he wore a cloak made from the beards of 28 kings of Britain whom he had defeated in battle. One day Rhitta heard that in the South at Caerleon a new King called Arthur had been crowned. It so happened that he needed only one more beard to make his cloak perfect.'

The Battle of Camlan – AD 537

'DID KING ARTHUR BRING PEACE TO BRITAIN, REALLY?'

'Indeed, he defeated the Saxons at the battle of Badon and there was a time of peace, but it was a peace won by war, and that kind of peace rarely lasts …'

Historians have long debated the site of Arthur's last great battle against his nephew Mordred (Mawdred) and his Saxon allies. Some claimed it was at Camelford in Cornwall, or Camelon in Scotland. Most recently it has been suggested that the battle took place at Cadlan on the Llŷn Peninsula of Wales. In old Welsh the word *cadgamlan* means a slaughter, so any of these sites might be the place of this final catastrophe.

A local historian, Thomas Davies, argued that the authentic Camlan was in the Dovey Valley at Dinas Mawddwy where Maes Camlan lies beneath the hillside of Craig y Gamell. Further up the valley in Cwm Cerist the A470 to Dolgellau crosses Bwlch Oerddrws to pass beneath another hill named Camlan where the battle may have begun, and only 5 miles to the east is Nant y Saeson, the valley of the Saxons, where Mordred's allies were said to have camped before the battle.

Wherever the battle was fought, it marked the end of this phase of Celtic resistance to the Saxons and both documentary and archaeological evidence shows that after 537 the Saxons occupied the Midlands and the south west of England. The British tribes retreated into their hill forts in Gwent, Powys and Gwynedd or bought an uneasy peace with the Saxons with tribute and treaties.

A view of Maes Camlan from Bryn Cleifion looking across Dol-y-Cleifion (the field of the wounded men) to Nant y Gamell (the crooked stream) which flows down to the River Dovey at this point.

Avalon

'WHERE WAS THIS PLACE AVALON?'

'That's a symbolic place, a kind of magical island where you could go for a rest; the happy other world.'

The old Celtic concept of the 'other world', a parallel universe where pagan gods and magic ruled, was readily adapted into the Christian idea of paradise. In Welsh the Isle of Avalon is called Ynys Afallach which means 'island of apples', and in Welsh tradition Merlin and Taliesin took the dying Arthur across the sea to this land of fruitfulness and plenty where he might be restored to health. Recent research identifies this island as Bardsey Island, off the western tip of the Llŷn Peninsula where St Cadfan retired, after founding a church in Tywyn, to establish a monastery between 516 and 542. This island is clearly visible across Cardigan Bay from the mouth of the River Dovey or from the hills above, and was renowned in the Middle Ages as the burial place of 1,000 Welsh saints. It is visited still by boat, crossing the narrow straits seen from the mainland in the view below.

The Cave Where Arthur Sleeps

'ONCE, A LONG TIME AGO ... THERE WAS A YOUNG MAN FROM WEST WALES WHO FOUND THE CAVE WHERE KING ARTHUR SLEEPS WITH ALL HIS KNIGHTS, WAITING FOR THE DAY WHEN HE WILL AWAKE AND RIDE OUT TO BRING JUSTICE TO A TROUBLED WORLD. THIS IS WHAT THE YOUNG MAN SAW ...'

The legend that a lost leader lives on and will come again to save the nation is common in the folklore of early cultures whether in Asia, America or Europe. Norse war leaders and Celtic kings were often reputed to have recovered from their wounds and could be 'resurrected' in time of need. The cave where Arthur sleeps has been variously identified in Brittany at Le Camp d'Arthus, in Edinburgh at Arthur's Seat, in County Durham at Arthur's Tor, on the Island of Anglesey, at Whitchurch near Hereford, and at several locations in Snowdonia.

Arthur also 'lives on' in British literature and mythology. The old Celtic tales of Arthur were retold in the Middle Ages by Geoffrey of Monmouth and by the Norman poet Robert Wace who introduced the Round Table as an emblem of feudal order. Malory's *Le Morte d'Arthur* drew on the Arthurian tradition as a model of medieval chivalry and religious values, and Henry Tudor, when he took the crown in 1485, sought to establish his descent from the heirs of Arthur. Each wave of occupation or oppression has invoked Arthur in its own interest but the memory of Arthur is most authentically celebrated in the Celtic culture from which it derives. Thus it is in Scotland, Ireland, Cornwall and Brittany, but especially in Wales that the tales of Arthur are told and retold; no knight in shining armour, no imperial monarch or emperor, no Holy Grail and no Round Table. The Celtic Arthur is now, as he always was, a warlord, a leader of the Welsh tribes in their years of resistance to invasion and an inspiration that has sustained the Celtic nations in their last strongholds on the western fringe of Europe.

Snowdon, where some historians locate Arthur's last battle at Bwlch-y-Saethau (Pass of the Arrows). The cave where Arthur's knights sleep is said to be on nearby Lliwedd.

The Mabinogion

... AN OLD, OLD BOOK FULL OF WONDERFUL TALES ...

The book known to the Welsh as *The Mabinogion* is a collection of stories which evolved over 1,000 years. The stories were passed from generation to generation by bards and story-tellers from the 4th century onwards, but were not written down in a surviving manuscript form until the 13th century. The *White Book of Rhydderch* (1325) and the *Red Book of Hergest* (1400) between them contain 11 stories. The four tales known as the *Four Branches of the Mabinogi* are set in an imaginary magical world of early Celtic myth and two other tales tell of half-remembered history at the time of the Roman occupation. The five remaining tales centre around the exploits of King Arthur and his contemporaries. It is in these tales that we first hear of Arthur's queen, Gwenhwyfar (Guinevere) and read the names of the warriors who later became knighted in the medieval romances: Cei (Sir Kay), Bedwyr (Sir Bedivere), Peredur (Sir Percival), Gwalchmei (Sir Gawain).

The Legend of the Lost Lands of Cantre'r Gwaelod

Gwyddno Garanhir ruled the lowlands to the west of Wales. The land was so fertile it was said that any acre was worth four acres elsewhere, but it depended upon a dyke to hold back the sea. At low tide the sluice gates were opened to drain water from the land and closed as the tide returned. One night Seithenin, the night-watchman, drank too much wine and fell asleep just as a gale from the south west drove the seas into Cardigan Bay. The water gates were left open and the sea rushed in. The land and all 16 villages of the cantref were flooded. Gwyddno Garanhir and his followers were forced to leave the lowlands and make a poorer living in the hills and valleys of Wales.

Taliesin

'I GREW UP TO BE A BARD, A STORY-TELLER, A SINGER OF SONGS AND MY NAME IS TALIESIN AND I WAS ALIVE IN THE TIME OF KING ARTHUR – GIVE OR TAKE A STORY OR TWO.'

Bards like Taliesin kept these stories alive and took pride in remembering every name and detail of the elaborate sagas. On the tidal flats of the River Dovey near the village now called Tre Taliesin stood a willow woven weir or fish trap in which the leather bag carrying the baby Taliesin was found by Elfin, the son of Gwyddno Garanhir some time after the inundation of Cantre'r Gwaelod. In an age of infanticide and abandoned infants this was a common enough explanation for a new baby in the household. This Taliesin was known to be alive around 580–600 and could not have been that same Taliesin who survived the campaign against Matholwch in Ireland in the 1st century and helped carry the head of Bran to the 'White Mount in London'. Nor is it likely that he could have been that Taliesin who, with Merlin, accompanied Arthur to Avalon.

Taliesin, then, like Merlin and perhaps like Arthur himself, was reincarnated in literature, as in life, in different times. The poems and stories of 'Taliesin' were remembered and embroidered by the bards who followed. How better to give authority to bardic tales of the 7th, 8th or 9th centuries than to attribute them all to Taliesin?

This ancient forest lies between Tywyn and Aberdovey. Among the medieval peat diggings are still to be found the tree stumps and roots of this sunken land. Perhaps here is the source of the legend of the lost lands of Cantre'r Gwaelod in the Celtic imagination.

The Caverns of Braich Goch Mountain

The vast caverns of King Arthur's Labyrinth are the surviving workings of the Braich Goch Slate Mine which operated between 1836 and 1970. The early years were difficult and four different companies failed before the opening of the Corris Railway in 1859 and the establishment of the Braich Goch Slate Quarry Co. in 1864.

The slate of the Appendix Vein was formed from Ordovician mud deposits, 500 million years ago. Metamorphosed by volcanic action and folding, it is very dense and pure, especially suitable for slab production. Miners of the 19th century drove access tunnels into the hillside until they reached this vein of high-quality slate, then turned at right angles to follow it in both directions. Shorter tunnels were driven across the vein to develop a series of chambers or caverns up to 50 metres wide and 25 metres high, separated by pillars of slate left to support the roof above.

In King Arthur's Labyrinth the boat takes visitors in on the old Level 6 tramway that was opened around 1850 and flooded in 1994 to create river access to the Labyrinth. Chambering into the higher Level 5 can be clearly seen above the Dinas Emrys chamber, while the Bran and Cantre'r Gwaelod chambers are linked behind the pillar to form a continuous roof of 50 by 100 metres, the size of a football pitch.

In 1878 the quarry employed 250 men and produced 7,000 tons of slab and roofing slate, but rising costs and falling demand saw the company collapse in 1906. Another five companies worked the mine intermittently until 1962 when it was bought by brothers Dewi and Gwilym Lloyd of Aberllefenni. For eight years high-quality slab was extracted for use as panels for electrical fittings, before a new road scheme brought the levelling of the slate tips, the closure of the slate mill and the building of the Corris Craft Centre on the reclaimed land in 1983.